Timeless

TRUE TREASURE

A.F. Foster

ISBN 979-8-88644-706-4 (Paperback)
ISBN 979-8-88644-707-1 (Digital)

Covenant Books
11661 Hwy 707
Murrells Inlet, SC 29576
www.covenantbooks.com

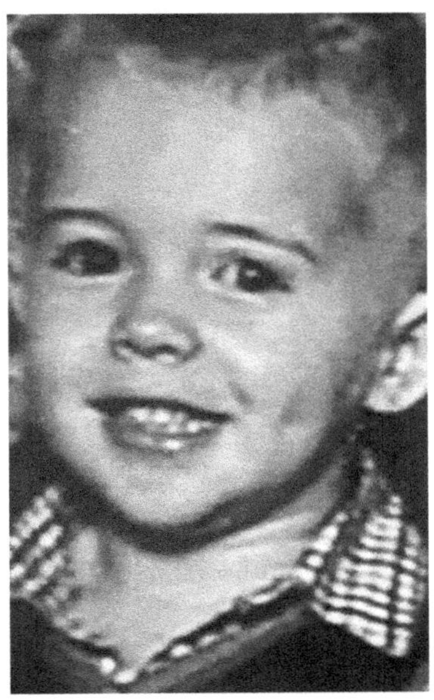

Nickolas

August 2012–June 2015

For where your treasure is, there your heart will be also.
—Matthew 6:21

This book is only three chapters. However, God directed me to write it as such. If you read all scriptures referenced throughout the text, there's so much more to behold. My prayer is that you'll look up each scripture, as it is referenced, so you might have the experience that's intended therein. Enjoy the timeless journey God has set before us. Keep your Bible handy; you will need it. I pray God blesses you.

Chapter 1

THE DIRECTOR

Who's directing your life? The origin of the word *director* is Latin meaning "to guide," whether it be the director of a company or some sort of a production, ultimately the director guides. We are going to explore what the role of a director is, in general, as it pertains to filmmaking. This explanation is paraphrased from a few of my Google searches:

> A film director controls the artistic and dramatic aspects and visualizes the script while guiding the technical crew and actors in the fulfilment of that vision. The director has a key role in choosing the cast members, production design, and all the creative aspects of filmmaking.

I'm not going to belabor this. My point is far more spiritual related than the listed roles of film directors. I just wanted to give a brief outline for explanation in comparison as I explain to you that the Holy Spirit is the director of my life. He's actually the director of life. Yes, we all have a part in life no matter how it's spun. The story has been written; the Holy Spirit is the director, Jesus is the main character and hero, and God is the author.

I have given you a glimpse into this plot, so now we will get back to this particular chapter in which the Holy Spirit is the main focus.

The Holy Spirit has a grand role in "His story." He is our director and protector. He guides us and helps us navigate our roles in living by cultivating our potential and gifts. The Holy Spirit is mentioned all throughout the Bible. He is on scene from the beginning (Genesis 1:1–2). The Holy Spirit was involved with the Author/Creator from the beginning as we know it. This book is titled *Timeless* because the origin of "His-story" is just that, timeless. Imagine eternity.

Take a moment to seriously pause and think about what eternity means. It is listed as "infinite or unending time." *Infinite* is listed as being "limitless or endless"; "impossible to measure or calculate." Just imagine! Or can you? I can't seem to comprehend this fully in application.

The Holy Spirit is beyond what we could ever imagine, think, or feel, etc. He is infinity and beyond. *Wow*! Check 1 Corinthians 2:11. With this scripture in mind, we can rest assured that the Holy Spirit is the best director we could hope for. I'm going to take you to some scenes from my own personal life film to give some applications as to how the Holy Spirit is indeed the director.

My life account started in my mother's womb. Yes, I said in my mother's womb, and yes, the Holy Spirit knew me even before and as I was formed (Jeremiah 1:5; Isaiah 49:5; Romans 8:29; Psalm 139:1–24).

Unfortunately, after I was born into this sinful world, my childhood was not the greatest. I have several unfavorable memories. I had many suicidal ideations (thoughts) and even came close to committing suicide. I had a moment at age 15 where a shotgun was accessible and God intervened. I had planned and even wrote letters saying goodbye on another occasion, and God again intervened.

The Holy Spirit has moved upon me, and also others to help me in my lifetime, unfailingly. There's no way to discount His presence's direction in my accounts of living. In these accounts, there are bad characters just as there are good characters. However, I would like to point out that for me, in my story, Jesus Christ, my hero, the main character, and the Holy Spirit, director, have always been present. God. the author, is omnipresent through infinity and beyond—timeless.

I didn't always recognize His presence or direction. I often questioned if He was still there, especially during the most difficult scenes of my life. This brings to mind a poem I have hanging in my house. It's a great reminder of what He once revealed to me.

Read this piece titled, "Footprints in the Sand" sometime. It's the first known version of which was written by Mary Stevenson, 1936. The Lord has often, through the inspirational direction of the Holy Spirit, brought verses to mind with which I can envision Him holding me with His righteous right hand and never leaving nor forsaking me (Isaiah 41:13; Psalm 18:35).

To Matthew Henry's commentary, Isaiah 41:13 displays:

> A promise that God will strengthen—
> He will take us by the hand as our guide to
> lead us in our way; will help us up when
> we're fallen or prevent our falls; when we
> are weak, He will hold us up; wavering,

He will fix us; trembling, He will encourage us, and so hold us by the right hand.

The Holy Spirit has surely guided me just as He has so many others throughout eternity, a gentle yet strong influence in my life. I have had many experiences to validate His genuineness. I have been comforted, convicted, reassured, interrupted, and so much more.

The memories of recent and past events are scarce for me, and the scientific/diagnostic explanation that I have been given for this is that I have post-traumatic stress disorder with memory blocking as part of my self-preservation techniques. Unfortunately, all my memories—long-term, short-term, good, and bad—have been affected.

I do know that the Holy Spirit has allowed me to navigate as I need to throughout life. I sometimes get frustrated and think, *Why must all my memories be affected?* I then realize that my mind is so very complex in its makeup and God is its Creator. He knows more than I ever could. I move along knowing that the director is near and available at all times even when I can't remember or (what might even possibly be worse) when or if I do remember. Can you imagine being afraid to remember yet being upset that you can't? It's unexplainable. The Holy Spirit has been with me through all the events of my life, remembered or not.

I often like to take pictures because they help my memory. I am going to give some short glimpses of my life from as early as I can remember, which is about age 4–5.

I remember dancing on the feet of my brother Dave to the song "Crimson and Clover." I have a feeling of comfort with that memory. I have another memory of him that has a scared, confused, and upset feeling that is attached to it. This stems from a time when my mom and I were lying on the couch for a daytime nap. We heard a very loud pop (my mom has been hard of hearing from her childhood). After this, I heard a faint "help me" coming from upstairs in our apartment. I shook my mom and told her. Following behind her, we went upstairs.

Once we went into the room, I remember my mom saying, "Oh my God, Dave, you didn't." She held on to the wall, appearing very weak in the knees, and went down the steps barely able to walk, and wailing (a noise I had never heard), she dialed for help on our kitchen wall phone.

Shortly after this, my dad came in while the EMTs were still there, and he went with my brother to the hospital. Dave was Life-Flighted to a larger area hospital but did not survive due to the loss of blood. It was the day after Christmas, and my brother had shot himself. Tragic! My mom knew a preacher that had assured her that he'd spoken with my brother and believed that he was right with God before taking his last breath (this was a comfort to our family that could only come from the Holy Spirit). That's the feelings I have associated with my brother Dave.

My mom had a very difficult time during Christmas for many following years. Her pain lingered and was associated with that time of year because the decorations were still up when it happened. There's a saying that says you may not remember exactly what was said or done but you'll remember the feeling that's associated with a who, what, when, how, or where. I find that my emotional, physical, and even spiritual senses bring certain people or encounters to mind for me that are associated with feelings I've felt.

The feelings associated with our senses (sight, smell, hearing, tasting, and touch) are often remembered more than the actual events which caused the feelings. Like when I was scalded with hot water from the neck down when I tipped the kettle up to see if there were any more hot dogs.

I remember the physical pain of the burn, yet also I remember hearing some people laughing in the background (I am not completely sure who this was, but it may have been some of my older siblings on a high). I came to know what pot smelled like at an early age. I knew to make myself scarce, and pretended as if I didn't smell it.

I have another memory of skating in shoe skates (the kind that didn't come up around your ankles). I twisted my ankle and have a scar on my right foot because of it, which is a physical reminder for me.

Another time, at this same apartment, I remember swinging on a swing that was actually a bicycle inner tube that was put on the metal clothesline pole. The swing broke, and the part of the tube where you air it up flipped up and hit me in the head, causing a small hole into my skull which bled like crazy (because it was a head injury, and they usually do). My mom wet a dish towel and held it tight to my head. I had to get stitches and still have a cowlick to this day because of that incident—another physical reminder. These things occurred before I ever accepted Christ as my Savior around age 8–9.

I was young and inexperienced in my faith, so I thought that the first time I messed up, God was mad at me, and I was lost again. I do, however, recall having a sort of knowing that I was different. My conscience was pretty tender. I didn't understand, but I had some restraint in certain areas of my life (in which many others I was around didn't seem to have). It was exhilarating but also somewhat frustrating at times. It seemed as if God's standards for me (in my life) were different, much like they still are today. I now know a bit more and better understand that the promptings of the amazing Holy Spirit have been with me all along! Still exhilarating yet occasionally frustrating—it's all good (Romans 8:28).

We moved from the apartment into a house in the country. I wish I could say things took a turn for the better, but they did not. My dad had many struggles in his early years with alcohol, and my older siblings drank. It's apparent to me that, often, mental health issues are hereditary. My dad and eldest brother sometimes would get drunk and fight. On one occasion, I remember we had to hide the gun and shells in separate places because they were threatening to kill each other.

One night, I needed to pee really badly; I heard noises and could smell the odor of alcohol, so I peeked out just before I opened the curtain from our bedroom, then I coughed and put my head down as if I hadn't seen one of my brothers and a sister that were on the couch and appeared to be making out.

Another time, another brother (who was hiding out near our house because he was accused of stabbing a man to death in a bar fight) had tried to take me into the bathroom while my parents were gone. I remember kicking him and running outside to my eldest brother's camper until my parents came back home. On another occasion, at some point around that time, my sister said she was beaten up and left to die in the creek down the road from our house. The police arrested my brother who was hiding out near our house on the murder charge after they and their dogs came through the woods around our house to track him down. They had found him hiding in a neighbor's building. He went to prison for many years.

On another occasion, while living at this house, the police came to our house one night, woke my mom and told her that my sister Diane had been struck by a car and died in front of "Lucky Lady" bar. Ironic and tragic! This occurred on the Fourth of July—again, another death associated with a holiday.

There was also a time when we lived at this home that me and some relatives of approximately the same age did sexual experimenting when camping out in tents and then another time when we had a stay over. I don't quite understand these things and probably never fully will. I have come to know that it's a fallen, sinful world we live in, and there has always been an enemy in my story and yours also (John 10:10).

He wants to kill, steal, and destroy, and the younger we are when he can start invading our minds, the more troubles we'll experience in this life. All throughout Scripture, we can see that sins are visited from generation to generation. In my story, I was born on a certain date to a certain people, but that's not all that affects my story just as my children being born to me and theirs to them.

All generations absolutely play a role in each story, but to be honest, our ancestors of way before and the generations of generations to come are inadvertently, or perhaps a better term are unknowingly, involved in one another's stories. The enemy's main goal is to destroy God's people with ignorance. The Holy Spirit is here to guide and protect and try to direct "the actors" (us) into the truth of the ongoing timeless adventure that we are taking part in.

We are all in an ultimate story/film of all time. We can either come in and read the script as it's handed to us or be as puppets on the enemy's strings (which is what the enemy wants because he doesn't want you or I to dare think we matter in this "film") or we can actually know the back-story and the direction the story has.

We can indeed know the end of the entire story, but we don't necessarily know every act we'll be part of and we won't know all the characters in our act/part of the story/film either. This is why we depend on the Holy Spirit as our director. We must show up and He tells us our part as it comes, sometimes in advance but sometimes not. He doesn't, however, expect us to be ignorant about the story in general (1 Peter 3:15).

We must be ready and on set for when our part is needed. You see, He's always there in the director's seat, and it's up to us if we want to have fun in our part or try to hide or take part in an "alternative" film in which the enemy deceives, derails, delays, or possibly destroys us. Ultimately, it's all the same feature film of all life. No matter where we think we should or could be, we are all part of His-story (Psalm 139). Our life story is ultimately written whether we want to participate or not. We are not puppets on a string, and God is not the puppet master, although that's what Satan would like to have us all believe. The devil has a counterfeit for everything and wants us to be afraid of

God, distrust Him, question Him and His character by deceptions—smoke and mirrors, so to speak.

Our God wants good for all people. He gave His Son for all, and it's unfortunate that many are not willing to except this. It's an aha moment—our part is to accept and to follow His direction so others might accept their part and follow also, and so on and so forth. It's a generational ongoing timeless truth that we all have a part in.

Do you really want to play the villain? Well, let me see. I guess you're right, the villains have been romanticized and glorified throughout the generations but only in man-made movies. His-story is clear about what happens to the villains. I don't personally want man-made, superficial, short-lived glory or romance in exchange for eternal gratification, glory, and honor in the presence of the author of the story/film Himself!

I would much rather hear the author say "well done" than have others in the story/film, the backstage, or audience give their approval. Believe it or not, we shouldn't be about the ratings. We should care much more about the grand feature and the overall outcome. You see, it's not only just this vapor of life in which we're playing part. It's the whole picture, all of it—timeless, eternal. Yes, my part absolutely matters, and so does yours. We aren't navigating in this feature all alone. We have our director (John 14:26; Matthew 10:19–20; Luke 12:11–12; 1 John 2:27; Nehemiah 9:20; Mark 13:11). He is prepared and always willing to direct us. Amazing! I am always amazed by how much God loves us.

I encourage you to read all referenced scriptures throughout this book. Scripture is the truth, and the truth will set you free. This first chapter is not the only place you will see our director, the Holy Spirit, mentioned because it's impossible for me to continue in the story without Him. I just basically wanted to give a chapter to explicitly explain some about Him in a context that I truly hope will help you to better understand Him. This book could never capture all the attributes and amazing, awesome wonders of the Holy Spirit. He's too grand to explain! We will leave this chapter now, but the Holy Spirit is coming along with us.

Mom and Dad

April 1935–November 2021, November 1921–January 2000

The Spirit Himself bears witness with our spirit that
we are children of God, and if children, then heirs of
God and joint heirs with Christ, if indeed we suffer
with Him, that we may also be glorified together.

—Romans 8:16–18

Chapter 2

CHARACTERS

Every story has a main character, and sometimes, the main character also happens to be the hero. Actually it happens very often but not always. The definition of the *main character* is the character that the story is mostly about or the point of view of the story. Who would you think is the main character in your story? My story? This story? His story? *Hmmm.* Can we tell? Let's take a closer look.

The answer to all these, I would suggest; you are, I am, we all are, and most importantly, He is (Jesus). Collectively and individually, we matter to our own story, this story, and His story. We all have been given a main character role. It amazes me how so many people will say things like, "If it's meant to be, it will be," "We're all dealt a hand and either we play or fold," "Our destiny is in our own hands" or "Our destiny is in His hands." There are many ways to think about life's script. There are so many, in fact, that it can become overwhelming at times. I have recently read this quote, "Human behavior flows from three main sources: desire, emotion, and knowledge" (Plato). I found this to be interesting and relevant to this chapter.

I decided to briefly research Plato since I chose to reference his quote, and he was, in my opinion, definitely a complex yet simplistic individual.

> Plato (born 428/427 BCE, Athens, Greece—died 348/347, Athens) was an ancient Greek philosopher, student of Socrates (c. 470–399 BCE), teacher of Aristotle (384–322 BCE), and founder of the Academy, best known as the author of philosophical works of unparalleled influence. (Internet Encyclopedia of Philosophy; Britannica)

As we see here with these fellows, we all have been given main character roles in our own story, others' stories, and His-story. Amazing how God works! Socratic Method—I wouldn't have any knowledge of who Socrates was had I not come across the quote of Plato, and how could I reference Plato and not include Socrates or Aristotle? *Timeless* is just that, timeless—beginning to end. Is this confusing, confounding, or all the above? I believe that this is a great example of how He works.

Jesus (our Hero) is the beginning and end (Revelation 21:6, 22:13; Isaiah 40:28; Psalm 90:2; Genesis 1:1). Our wants and desires may drive us, our experiences may prompt us, our emotions may lead us, or often our intellect may interpret for us, however, it's never been about us and yet it all involves us, unto His glory—very complex yet simple.

Our God is the Creator of all. He made us a "little lower than the angels," "sons and daughters," "brothers and sisters" (Hebrews 2:6–11). "The builder of a house has greater honor than the house itself," "God is the builder of everything," "We are His house" (Hebrews 3:3–6). We should only be led by the Holy Spirit in truth—His truth, not ours or others.

Does life matter? Have you ever asked yourself, "What am I doing here?" I most certainly have. I am still not completely sure that I have the right answer, but I have discovered some answers. Read these scriptures. and perhaps you'll have some answers also: Psalm 139:13–16, Jeremiah 29:11, Titus 3:4–8, Galatians 2:19–21, Romans 8:1–39,

Genesis 1:27, John 1:12–13, Ephesians 2:1–22, Luke12:7, and Matthew 16:26.

There are so many more scriptures that are relevant to these questions also—"Ask and you shall receive." As I said before, we must live life based on His truth and not just by our wants and desires, emotions, or intellect, etc. You see, we need the Word of God, Scripture, and His Holy Spirit in order to align our will with His. We have free will, so we have a part to be doing whether we want that responsibility or not. We must hold ourselves accountable as He leads us. He doesn't bring condemnation (the enemy/Satan does that), but He will bring conviction and correction. This is because He loves us so much that He wants us to be free. All God does or doesn't do on our behalf is ultimately for our own good and His glory. God's glory is to our good.

He is good—light (1 John 1). In light there's cultivation, growing, and thriving happening. Darkness brings deterioration, death, and destruction. There's a site listed below that has some insight with Bible verses to help explain this point:

> In the New Testament, "walking in the light" is directly related to following Jesus, who said, *"I am the light of the world. He who follows me shall not walk in dark-*

ness, but have the light of life" (John 8:12).
("What does it mean to walk in the light?" gotquestions.org)

Without Jesus, the overall story is void of light. The entire Bible points to Jesus. The life we live is truly only enlightened when we come to know who Jesus is. He is the Savior of the world!

Who wouldn't want to know this hero? Knowing more about Him guides us into a better fulfilling of our own roles. Ultimately, we are all in the story for eternity. I have heard it said, "This physical life is just a dress rehearsal for what's to come." We all are living out our roles, and as we're utilized in different roles in our life experiences, they are all important roles. Some are for a season, and others are lifetime roles—grandparent, daughter, son, brother, sister, friend, coworker, teacher, nurse, etc. The list goes on and on, yet I believe one of the most important roles one will ever be given is that of being a parent—father, mother—or grandparent. A parent's role extends beyond just their children into their children's children and generation to generation. It's a great responsibility and privilege.

The Bible is clear to me that all our choices have consequences, some good and some bad. Also, what we do or don't do affects people from generation to generation

(Psalm 78:8, 105:8, and 145:4 and 13; Exodus 20:5–6 and 34:6–7; Deuteronomy 5:8–10 & 7:7–10; Matthew 24:32–34; Acts 2:40; Daniel 4:3, see <u>80 Bible verses about Generations (knowing-jesus.com)</u>).

I am so amazed at God's sovereign grace and will be forever grateful. Everywhere I look in life, there is overwhelming evidence of God our Creator. I think it's okay to say Jesus is the main character, and yet He's also in the authorization and writings of it all, all creation. Ultimately, we are here to be loved by God, our Creator, and to love one another as He loves us. The key here is in knowing the love of our heavenly Father. It's not just something He does, nor is it conditional; it's who He is. Our complex yet simplistic being is an amazing mystery.

The Bible has every type of story we could imagine. Investigate it for yourself. I would suggest having an enthusiastic approach and praying for the Holy Spirit to read it "aloud" with you.

> Those who have ears to hear, let them hear. (Matthew 11:15 and 13:9; Mark 4:9 and 4:23)

It's difficult to seek revelation without revelation. We must have faith that Jesus is the author and finisher of our faith (Hebrews 12:2). Hebrews 1–4 has some more insight with many revelations to behold. Reading anywhere in the Bible can give more insight as we read, but it's important to pray for revelation from the Holy Spirit.

Hebrews has insights of how Old Testament scripts point to the real thing—Jesus. It's apparent that there can be many interpretations of Scripture, but we have to be diligent in seeking the author's interpretation because what could ever be a better interpretation than that of the author? His intent and purpose are why we read the book. His book, the Holy Bible, is like no other—it's living Word. Reading the Bible is a life-changing, sustaining, and an enlightening experience. Our roles become ever clearer as we get to know His purpose. He has many roles through-out the story, as do we.

It's amazing to me just how relevant and personal an Almighty God has been willing to become in His quest to be in a relationship with each of us. Father, Son, and Holy Spirit are all-in-one. Jesus is everything. He loves us all— you, me, our family, our friends, our coworkers, the entire population. We each have a part, and at some point in the story, we will get to be the main character (not the hero— Jesus is the only human hero). The best way to be properly equipped to play our part is to come to know the author, the story line, and the purpose of each of our own roles. We are all individuals of a greater picture. Apart from Him, we can do nothing (John 15:5). He's our light and life. Who are we that He would be mindful of us? (Psalm 8:4–8).

With all these amazing attributes of God, there is still yet a rebellious nature in us because of free will, which brings me to the fall of Satan. In his arrogance and self-ishness, he wanted to exalt himself above his Creator. This caused a division between the Creator and created, what we call good and evil. You see, God is Father, Son, and Holy Spirit—three in one. He is entirely good! Satan, on the other hand, is entirely evil. He's the father of lies. He is counterfeit.

In 1 Peter 5:8, we see that he is like a roaring lion. He's not a roaring lion. Jesus, our Christ, is the Lion of Judah. Satan preys on the weak, and here, Peter warns us to be sober-minded. We must shield our thoughts from the lies of the devil with the truth of God's Word; be alert and watchful so we can catch Satan at his onset before he has influence in our minds. Satan has helpers, but neither he nor they are omniscient like God. They don't have the power that God, His angels, and God's people have. We're all given free will. We get to decide what we're going to do with the life we're given. Ultimately, our best option is to be in a relationship with God. We have a choice to follow His Word and direction or our own way and Satan's deceptions.

Pride is probably the greatest of Satan's attributes. Pride is very deceptive in itself. It can be good as with dignity and self-respect but bad when twisted even just a little as one then teeters on indignancy and then falls into one's own selfish desires rather than that of the common good, or even more importantly, the glory of God, our Creator.

Let's be of one mind (Philippians 2:2–8). Satan is indeed our enemy, the villain. Jesus is the hero. We are not only reading the script but also participating in the unfolding of the story. Scripture will help us as we live out our roles. Here are a few to look up: Ephesians 6:10–11; 2 Corinthians 10:4–5; 1 Peter 5:8–9; James 4:7–8; Romans 8:37–39; John 10:10; Colossians 1:13–14; John 16:33; 1 Corinthians 10:13; 2 Thessalonians 3:3. I hope these have encouraged you to keep up the good fight of faith (1 Timothy 6:11–16).

There are so very many "actors" throughout His-story. All serve a purpose as we all have a part to play. Never discount your meaning in this world or eternity. You and I are involved in this timeless work of art whether we're purposeful and intentional participants or not. Free will and predestination are both biblical. We are all predestined in this timeless drama, so to speak. It's our own free will that determines how we choose to act out our part. I am going to take you through an example to give some analogies of what I believe our part as characters is in this grand feature. I will be using something that actually became quite interesting to me as I took some time to look into it.

The Holy Spirit's prompting brought me to use this analogy related to a time when my husband decided he was going to use J-B Weld on his chainsaw. He was preoccupied with some other things, so he applied only one of the two parts. Those of you who know anything at all about J-B Weld will know that without both parts, the resin and the hardener, it will not work its intended purpose. My husband later came in laughing and said that he didn't know why he did that because he knew better.

There are so many lessons in this little mishap that I couldn't resist as the "director" guided me to give account of each one. The resin without the hardener is basically useless especially in this case, because my husband's goal was to weld the part on the saw. That couldn't happen without both parts being mixed and applied. The parts didn't stick together because the resin was applied but there was no hardener—useless.

I looked *resin* up, and this is what I found, relatively speaking: resin is flexible and needs to be able to adapt to the contents when the weight or volume changes. Resin is the great impersonator! Our opportunities are only limited by our imagination. Resin is versatile and can serve many purposes. How does this correlate with our acting analogy? Well, I am glad you asked. It's fascinating to me. Our scenes change day by day and even moment to moment, so we should be like resin—flexible, adaptable, and versatile. In a sense, actors are impersonators (Galatians 6:7–9). They impersonate the character which they have been called/assigned to play.

As Christians, we are called to follow Christ—impersonate, to assume or act the character of Christ. We should follow His example and act like Him to the best of our ability. The roles will change throughout the whole story, but nevertheless, the actor has a part in each particular section of their character roles. We are all involved in the story of life. It's completely (free will) up to us who we will "impersonate" (Joshua 24:1–28). Character is qualities that make us distinct from one another. Our individuality is displayed in our character.

What character do you want people to see in you or remember about you? Jesus is the ultimate model for all Christians. After all, Christian means to be Christlike. God and the Holy Spirit are like the hardener—God molds us, and the Holy Spirit solidifies. We aren't complete without all three of them. All in One working to bond and strengthen us.

God's vision is beyond our sight.

Chapter 3

THE AUTHOR

Good—adj, having the qualities required for a particular role. n, that which is morally right;—righteousness. v, benefit or advantage to someone or something

Omni—all; of all things

Dad—father, to father, to create. Uniquely the law giver to his chosen people (as in founding fathers) (*Oxford Language Dictionary*)

(See 2 Corinthians 6:18; Ephesians 4:6; Psalm 103:13; Proverbs 3:11–12.)

He created all. He divides good and bad. He sees the good and forgives the bad. The bad is cast out, and the good is brought forth. He made a way for us to be reconciled to Him even before we knew we needed to be reconciled. He sees and knows all. Wow! This can be scary if we're doing the wrong things and don't know the love of God, but it's exciting when we know the love of God and are trying to do the right things. He's there to help us through it all. His promises are true. He's always good (Psalms 25:8–10, 34:8, 100:5, 119:68, 145:9; James 1:17;1 Chronicles 16:34; Nahum 1:7; Mark 10:18).

Only God! He's the One who wrote the script! If He didn't care, why would He give us instructions? *Hmmm.* Think about that. It's unimaginable why He cares so much. I am just so very thankful that He does. The Word of God gives us a very clear picture of who God is and what He wants—He's all good and wants all good for us.

The whole Word of God reveals His purpose and plan, which is for us to have a relationship with Him (John 4:23–24; Psalms 139:7, 143:10; 2 Corinthians 3:17–18; Acts 7:48–50, 17:24; 1 Timothy 6:15–16).

God is Spirit. He's Holy and God—a God of goodness who will not allow evil into His holy presence (it will burn up in hellfire). His Scripture is clear and divides good from evil. Therefore, if He was not clear about this, then He wouldn't be truthful. A good Father directs, guides, instructs, warns, loves, comforts, etc. He is the perfect Father. Ultimately, He is the *all.* Everything we'll ever need, want, or desire lies within our relationship with Him. It's such an amazing process in which we get to participate in. I'm still trying to grasp why He loves me so much! It's supernatural and so beyond measure that I'm not sure that I will ever grasp it.

We all must have our own personal revelation of the redemptive restoration that God offers each of us. This doesn't mean that we're set apart to our own exclusive personal relationship with Him, but it means we're set apart to Him—meaning we're all as believers set apart to and for Him. It's a family unity revering their Father. It's so important to know God on each level of who He is to get a clear and balanced revelation to enhance our relationship with Him. God provides it all personally and collectively (Revelation 3:20). Open up to Him. We all need God. Creation without a Creator is not possible.

Creation was tainted by sin and evil, so therefore we all are subject to sin and evil, but God has given us a way out. He knew so He made provision. If we try to figure it all out, then we're clearly not trusting Him. In every relationship, there must be trust (Psalms 28:7, 37:34, 56:4; Isaiah 26:3; Proverbs 29:25).

God is Creator of all and Father to those who accept Him as Lord. God speaks, and sometimes it's unclear in that moment, but He always gives an answer in His time. Those who have ears to hear, let them hear and eyes to see, let them see what the Lord says (1 John 3:20; 2 Peter 3:8–9; Ecclesiastes 3:1–8). God gave us physical, emotional, and spiritual feelers.

I'm going to share with you some more of the many experiences that I've had associated with the parting of loved ones. There are some tangible and intangible things that are associated with each that bring back the feelings experienced with the memories. These are only a few more accounts of the many I have experienced throughout my life. One is when my brother Mike died in an accident. He reportedly crossed the median and hit a tractor trailer head-on. There was no explanation as to what caused this accident, so there were many speculations. His funeral was a closed-casket service as it was with my sister Diane, who passed when I was around twelve years old. Because the funerals were closed-casket services, it almost did not seem real that either were gone.

I was nineteen when Mike passed. I remember the smell of diesel fuel permeating from the casket when we were at the graveside service. I was very unsettled concerning the manner of his death, and God was gracious. He gave me some closure as I had a dream that Mike was actually in the air above, looking on at the very moment when the impact of the accident occurred. This gave me comfort in which only God could provide.

My dad passed when I was twenty-seven. It was expected but all at the same time unexpected. He had congestive heart failure. I had become remarkably close with my dad. My mom and I were the ones who cared for him. I was devastated, to say the least, when he passed. I drank a lot more in the months following, trying to mask the pain of grief. I remember I was startled when the honor guard shot off rounds at his graveside service, which snapped a response in me of uncontrolled crying. I was helped by someone to return to our vehicles, but on our way there, a horse came to the fence with a beautiful calming effect that instilled a comfort that "it's going to be okay, he's okay." God had once again given a peace and comfort that only He could provide.

The next one I've chose to mention is Nickolas, our step grandson. He passed just a couple months shy of turning three. I was forty-one. This was new territory for me. I couldn't imagine, and to be honest, I was angry with God for some time. We were called by our son, saying, "Pray for Nickolas. He drowned. They're still working on him."

I still cry at the recollection of this horrific event in life. Tears still stream as I write. He was only a part in our lives for a short time but left such an imprint on my heart that is unexplainable. I knew when I first met him that there was something uniquely special about him, beyond my comprehension. When we received the call from our son, we were on our way home, and I immediately started a prayer chain with our church. I will never forget I went straight to our bedroom and dropped to my knees, pleading to God for him to make it, then suddenly, God "spoke" and imparted a knowing within me that "he's home now."

I can't explain the overwhelming gush of pain that flooded over me. Just then, God spoke again to my spirit, saying, "Pray! Pray for Micha, pray for Codey, Nickolas's daddy, grandparents, all his family because this pain is multiplied for them in this moment and they need prayers."

Obeying God, I prayed and prayed. Then I asked others to pray. Only God can bring comfort in this. I knew this from experience but was still not grasping it. There are several things I remember about going through the process of his passing and memorial services. I am only going to mention a couple of things currently, but mostly it involved praying so very often. God prompted me to make up an arrangement of flowers for his service, and a butterfly was part of this arrangement, so I researched symbolism related to the butterfly because I knew God had chosen it to be there for a reason.

I learned that in symbolism, "butterflies are deep and powerful representations of life. They are beautiful and have mystery, meaning, and are a metaphor representing spiritual rebirth, transformation, change, hope, and life. The magnificent, yet short life of the butterfly closely mirrors the process of spiritual transformation and serves to remind us that life is short" (gardenswithwings.com).

Life stands out to me. Jesus lives, so I know that Nickolas lives also. A scripture reference, Isaiah 57:1, was on his memorial card, and with that, I believe God was sparing his innocence. I don't pretend to understand, I choose to trust. I believe he is certainly a timeless treasure that will be forever in the presence of God. A very spiritual prayer warrior from our church gave us a gift afterward. It is an angel holding a teddy bear that says, "Those we have held in our arms for a little while we hold in our hearts forever." It has a butterfly on it. God continues to speak. Listen.

She also had a blanket with Psalm 34:18 sent to me when I had heart surgery repairing the mitral valve at age forty-four. She passed at age sixty-three related to cancer. I was forty-six. She had one of the most beautiful Holy Spirit-inspired and Holy Spirit-filled memorial services I have ever attended. She had a quote displayed that read, "God's vision is beyond our sight." What a wonderful insight. She had her memorial service planned from the songs that were played to the scripture she wanted our pastor to read. I now want to have mine planned as well. The most important thing that I want my loved ones to know when I pass is that I love them but Jesus loves them more. I want to spend eternity with Him and them.

My mom passed at age eighty-six on what would have been my dad's one hundredth birthday, the day after Thanksgiving. I was forty-seven. Losing my mom has a pain that's inexpressible, yet I also have a peace that surpasses understanding—a peace only God can provide. My mom actually started preparing me for her passing long before she passed. She knew where she would spend eternity and was ready when God called her home.

My brother and I were with her the morning she passed, and there was no real "special" thing that happened such as bright light or anything like that. I can say that I did, however, witness a single tear leaking from her eye. We were on each side holding her hands. I told her it was okay to leave us, and we would be okay until we were together once again. She was a great woman and the best mother. God gave me so much comfort throughout the process of her passing, memorial service, and thereafter. I recalled many things that my mom had said to me, and the sadness is curbed and replaced with the joy in knowing we will soon be together again in the sweet by-and-by.

Even though things had not already been put in place for her service, it went very smoothly and came together nicely. There was an article that my brother found and wanted to be read at her service, which was a blessing considering. The article is "When God Created Mothers" by Erma Bombeck. Read it and you will see what I am saying. God has given so many reassuring comforts, and I am so very thankful (Romans 8:35–39).

For I am persuaded that neither death nor life, nor angels nor principalities nor powers, nor things present nor things to come, nor height nor depth, nor any other created thing, shall be able to separate us from the love of God which is in Christ Jesus our Lord.

—Romans 8:38–39

Time is not our master! Don't allow carnality to limit your life. Eternity is beyond our physical, emotional, and intellectual senses (Hebrews 11). I pray that the Holy Spirit will open our hearts and minds to the eternal treasures that are timeless. I have just recently realized that God has been working through all the grief in my life. I knew He was present but did not realize the extent of His presence. You see, because He is omniscient, He is well capable to work in and through our lives to have great meaningful relationships that are impactful for all eternity.

My friend had a miscarriage a brief time after she was able to hear her baby's heartbeat. She was devastated. She held the pain and was upset long after. She had asked God to give her some comfort but seemed to receive none that helped her from the despair she was feeling. God placed her on my mind for prayer, but I had no idea of the struggle she was enduring. The enemy had been trying to destroy her just as he had me throughout my life. God revealed that He was using what the enemy had wanted to use to destroy me to instead prepare and enable me to be sensitive and minister love to others who were struggling with grief.

My now very dear friend was just an acquaintance at the time of our grandson, Nickolas's passing, but as I was praying for her, God reminded me of the hug she gave me. He had actually given me that hug through her heartfelt obedience to hug me in that moment even though we barely knew one another. You see, I received and gave many hugs in those days, but this was a special connection which God had formed in that moment. I had never even realized it until we started walking through her grief together and God revealed His amazing grace.

There is a great comfort with people who are there for you in times of trouble, pain, grief, or despair, but when God is involved, there is a different unexplainable comfort. He has made me realize that we must be obedient to Him when He prompts us to interact with others. I was going to list more of the events that happened in our journey, but some things are just between you and God. Because they are so incredible, it would be difficult to explain and would not be easily understood by others. Our life, no matter how trivial it may seem, has purpose and meaning. The author of our story says so (Jeremiah 29:11). I've found that as we navigate throughout our role in life, the only timeless treasure that will forever hold true is our relationships with God and with others—spiritual connections.

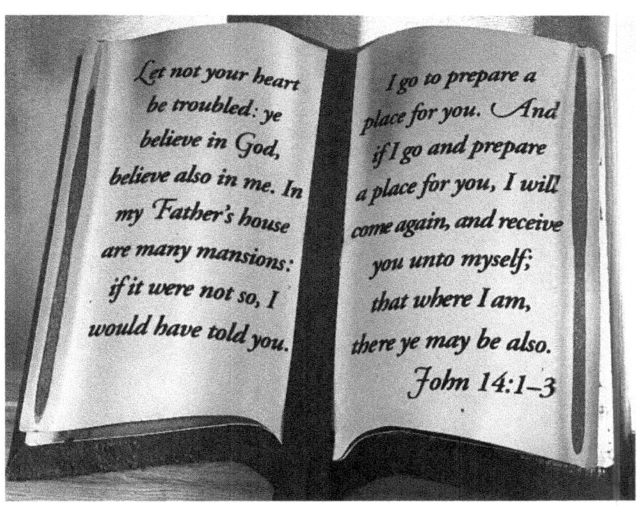

There's life beyond natural death.

NOTES

NOTES

43

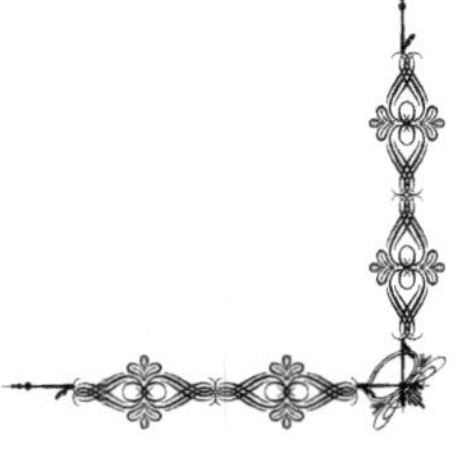

NOTES

NOTES

ABOUT THE AUTHOR

Foster is saved by God's grace. She has been given many roles throughout life: daughter, granddaughter, sister, niece, aunt, cousin, friend, mom, wife, grandma, waitress, retail worker, CNA, LPN, RN, now writer, etc. There were some other negative roles which she and the enemy had tried to appoint for her, but none would stick. She has learned that God has given her roles and seasons to live through, which have ultimately brought her closer to Him. Her life story has ups, downs, and turnarounds. She has learned that throughout it all, she's been God's girl (even when she has felt as if she had failed in her part). She would like to impart this revelation to her readers: God loves her, and He loves you. Really, it's real love!